GIRAFFES OF DEVOTION

SARAH MANGOLD

GIRAFFES OF DEVOTION

Sarah Mangold

KORE PRESS ⚓ TUCSON ⚓ 2016

standing by women's words since 1993
Kore Press, Inc., Tucson, Arizona USA
www.korepress.org

Cover art by Suzy Barnard, "Blue Dusk", 2009. www.suzybarnard.com
Cover design by Lisa Bowden
Design by Sally Geier

We express gratitude to the National Endowment for the Arts, the Tucson-Pima Arts
Council, the Arizona Commission on the Arts, and to individuals for support to make
this Kore Press publication possible.

ISBN: 978-1-888553-90-1

Library of Congress Cataloging-in-Publication Data

Names: Mangold, Sarah, author.
Title: Giraffes of devotion / by Sarah Mangold.
Description: Tucson : Kore Press, [2016]
Identifiers: LCCN 2015043478 | ISBN 9781888553901
Classification: LCC PS3563.A473 A6 2016 | DDC 811/.54--dc23
LC record available at http://lccn.loc.gov/2015043478

for Maggie, Lou, & Rammy

This is a description of a continent of living: lions, streetcars, explosions, newspapers like flies, flies like newspapers, giraffes of devotion, sentences in locomotion as contrived as giraffes, as devoted as all passing fashions. This is a description of passions designd as costumes of real living.

—Robert Duncan

CONTENTS

1900 1910s 1912 1913 1919
1920-1940s 1920s 1922 1925
1930s 1935 1937 a abroad
academy activities after
allowed

alone among ancestors and
and Annapolis Annapolis
Maryland as as at away back

battleship be because
bedroom born Boxer
Rebellion buff by by Captain
Phillip R. Alger Captain Roy
C. Smith III USNR Charleston
childhood children China

Didn't the Navy help out, help you

Certainly not what Navy
they had the Navy
purchasing office in Shanghai
which is no more good
to you than that sofa
not as good if you
want to sit on it
there was no no—so
anyway the next day
there we are
what to do
very agitating
I could leave the children aboard
ship because they were
six eight ten twelve
I could leave them aboard
ship because they had people
not nurses but you know
attendants of some sort women

Well, up to a point

But good-night
are you going to say
you won't enjoy a rose
because you might have
a lily the next day
not that I'm comparing

ourselves with roses and lilies
but I mean all right
are you not going to eat an oyster
because tomorrow you might have crab
I don't see the point
it's discouraging if they meet you like that

That's one of my difficulties

Well everybody had a cook in these days
            I couldn't imagine ever not
            having a servant in the house
            so I never did learn all the
            proper arts the
            d o m e s t i c   a r t s
            because we had duty away
        when we got to Newport
        the woman who used to be my cook
        in Annapolis her daughter
        married a sailor she was there
    She saw our name in the paper
    she rushed over and I had her

Chinamen climate comic command Commander Smith commanding commanding courts cousin date dates death December

demerits description dinner
dinner dinners drinking during
duty duty duty early early early
1900s early 1930s educated
education elaborate
experiences

In Shanghai

This scared me too
because you know
the price is going to escalate

we go down to dinner
we're sitting around a table
and in the middle of dinner a shooting

bang bang

some lady is brought in and laid on the floor
I could see her catercorner

Chinese lady

I don't know what kind
of a lady she was
No she wasn't as a matter of fact
I think she was French

        And Roy of course
        stuck under his seat

I grabbed him by the seat of the pants
                Sit down sit down
                you're not going out
                with a shooting

      I made him to his rage
      stay you see
      they brought her in

                Mrs. Doyen warned me be
                very careful not to let anybody
                eat anything except thus and so
                well-cooked you know

hazardous duty pay
hostile fire pay
career incentive pay

The Chinese all had umbrellas
and all had tea
and if it rained they stopped fighting
This is what the book says

He'd rented me three rooms

the third one reluctantly

he'd rented it to a young man who was out there
but gotten in a fight with a rickshaw coolie
and was in the hospital with a broken hand

I didn't know what these little points of light were
I couldn't imagine
  so I sat up in bed
  what is that
  who are you

        He'd got out
        and come back
        he thought home

he finds he had been invaded by us

so I said Beat it   Beat it   Go away
I don't know what became of him

exhausted again
I slept a little
the bed began doing this
I hung over the edge and looked

there was a coolie
all he was doing
he thought it was easier to get into the girls' room
and get their shoes to polish
but he was creeping

under the bed

to get to their room

to get to them

all he wanted were the shoes my shoes and the boys' shoes

family family's Far East father
February 1912 flu epidemic
food for formal friends friends
from future Georgia Georgia
USS (BB-15)

Glaucoma, was it

    Not glaucoma no what he turned out to have was that's in the
        muscles isn't it
    trachoma is a filth disease
    from pork isn't it
    no I think it's trichinosis
    no I think it's an infection
    no it's how you handle the rickshaw hurts your eye
    I see

We didn't feel we had to run

    The Admiral was there on duty I guess twice
    and she grew up there as a girl
    she knew all kinds of people

She would have liked me to have done a lot more
going around and calling becoming acquainted
with the elite but after all there is a busy life

getting the kids outfitted and oriented they had a terrible time with their lessons at first until they got fixed and loved to go swimming and we both loved to read we spent a lot of time peacefully but by that time of course it was in the future

get guest habits Hawaii he
health healthreasons health
her her her his his home
housing husband ill in in in
initially institute is Jr June
1925 to

February 1928 Kenneth
Whitings lack late late 1920s
leave Lieutenant Commander
Smith liquor Louisa Smith
Barnard love Luckenbach map
marries marries Mary

Home from Panama

And my daughter my other
daughter had one of those
quiet off-the-record marriages
you might say which gave
everybody 900 fits and then
Roy got himself out of the
Naval Academy for demerits
which nearly killed everybody
my youngest son had
appendicitis we were living in
an apartment on the second
floor the furnace was coal and
on the second floor and here's
my daughter home with a new
baby Monty had appendicitis
my husband was in the
hospital with high blood
pressure and I'm running the
furnace

How much time did your father spend at the Naval Institute

His week was divided he came and went I think he went to Washington twice a week perhaps but I don't really remember when you were growing up that was not part of your life actually no when you were growing up did you remember when your father went to the office or didn't go to the office or where he went and what he did we didn't pay any attention that was his—

my grandmother came and lived with us after a while and she was very serious minded so that the devil was down pa's home was up I ran around between them minding my own business

I must have been 14 15
And after that I came home
and stayed at home
and took French
and music lessons
in the ancient way
you know
you don't get educated
you get finished

It seems to me there was always a ship in the background and somebody worrying about it

He said this is terrible

This is awful
we saw him at a party well I'm not
saying he talked as free as that but I
mean that was the idea here is the fleet
all bottled up like this here and he was
going to complain bitterly to the
President he did go back and he got
transferred to another job

Alger Mary Alger Mary Smith
Staley mathematics meals
meets Memphis merchant ship
mid-1920s mid-1930s
midshipmen military benefits
and privileges moves Mrs.
Smith's Mrs. Smith's

music naval naval academy naval war college navigator navy new Newport Newport Rhode Island NOA Noa USS (DD-343) Noa not not of of officer officers Oglala Pacific area Panama Panama

Yes but not—

I used to play mah-jongg all the time with the
gals I've known in China

Yes some girls I've known here But the men
didn't play very much We used to play go
ashore and play at eleven o'clock and played
'till about five It was wonderful But otherwise
we didn't

I had a terrible time because I was not taking the liquor in those days and they'd say Now what will you drink Of course naturally my dear husband would drink whatever they offered him like most naval officers And I

said Nothing thank you And they would have a fit and say You must have something I'd say no no I'm not thirsty It doesn't make any difference you must have something This got to be terrible you know Then they started saying What will we give Mary to drink Can you feature

Because my daughter broke her arm

And that was fierce
I had taken the children
I had taken the Bernard children
and my children down to this sort of girl guide thing
She had broken her other arm two years before
at home and she broke her elbow before
It seemed to be here and there I was

Finally a man came up to me
and said Shanghai General Hospital is the best
He said can I do anything for you
I said yes you certainly can
You can take all these children home
He took them all off with him in a car
He had a car I got a rickshaw

It was race week and again we were popular as lepers

     They put Lou in a room
Of course you won't have a doctor until   you better take her home

     Meanwhile I began getting cold chills
          What have I done with the children
          Where did they go how do I know
          Who took them how do I know
          they took them home

     My only hope was he wouldn't do much
     he couldn't do much with six of them
     but still how did you know in this country
     where all sorts of things went on

I went fiercely down   stationed myself in the front hall
In comes a man who looked like a doctor
I fell upon him it turns out fortunately for me he's a bone fellow

He's coming entirely out of context

Just the right doctor

Yes he's out of context entirely

He's coming to see a patient

That's what you call Navy luck

We're all chief—what do you call it

    Chief engineers
        no the south—listen to me
        the pacific fleet
        commander in chief
        commander in chief pacific fleet
        no not the pacific fleet
        the asiatic fleet
        the asiatic fleet
            yes but as I said

parents parents participation
parties parties physical fitness
picked powder monkey
predicts private professor
prohibition proximity public
schools RADM

carriers are usually named
for famous men
ships of the old navy
or historic battles
destroyers for American heroes
and secretaries of the navy
cruisers for cities
submarines for fish
and other creatures of the sea
also for famous men

And naturally I wished to be very stylish

We had a woman come in and serve just serve
and this gal came over
and said she could serve
she was fine
and I thought well she's pretty good

She came over on the ferry just in time to serve dinner
and it was a new one
I didn't like her looks much
Oh yes she knew everything
Fine all right

She opened the door the pantry door swinging door
put her head in—Y'all want soup
I nearly died

Today I'm old and tough and would have laughed
In those days I nearly perished
Can you imagine

I kept hissing at her and she came off
she started to take the plates
stacked them to carry off
two or three at once
I almost perished

It was awful
but you could get perfectly civilized service
without any trouble really and truly

do not write or chart a course on the tablecloth
the less the incident is noticed the better

Avoid awkward positions with your hands at all times

Interesting things in every day living are always safe and non-controversial women are given desirable seats opposite each other at banquettes a man does not have to pay for the lunch or dinner at a chance encounter with a woman you may touch her arm lightly turn away as soon as you have accomplished your mission you may touch your hat when you rise to your feet a man should not ask an unknown woman to share a taxi but if he knows her slightly and if she's going his way

You had conversation my dear sir period

She certainly realized what problems she created for
the hostess

I don't think she cared
I don't know
I don't know
She used to go off on long trips

After he died
she went on that trip to Africa by herself
somebody asked her if she minded going by herself
she didn't mind at all

She was taken ill on that trip and died
taken somewhere in Africa to a hospital
but anyway she didn't have any children
I don't know what she would do

An old Chinese gentleman all dressed in gray silk
A Mandarin type
Well you know long gray silk gown and a black
A scholar type
They all wore fedora hats
no matter what else
and we rushed up to him

Wilson   ranking   receives
recollections rejected relative
resigns   retirement   Rizal
running rushes

Meanwhile Cam took command of the Noa up
in Chefoo

    and immediately ran into a typhoon
    the first typhoon he'd ever known

    The ship had been commanded by a classmate
    who thought it would be a good idea for Cam
    to take over in the middle of the typhoon
    If anything happened
                it wouldn't be his pigeon
                they had quite a time coming down

    They took green seas over the forecastle and broke out
    the glass in the bridge screen some of it

And in Chefoo, they still had a burial, a baby tower

It was not used I think if you had a girl baby
you went and dropped it down the tower but
the Catholic sisters established a large place
there and they took the babies they had an
orphanage well what they had was a workshop
really they took them and raised them up and
as soon as they were old enough to hold a
needle they taught them to do beautiful
embroidery and they sew wonderful
embroidered linens you see which was good
all around I don't know whatever happened to
the girls in the end their eyes gave out after
awhile well I don't know they probably got
married I don't know what they did

scares Mrs. Smith by sneaking
on train to Baltimore as young
child as child takes bones as
souvenir from Philippine
burial cave education
retirement Roy Roy Smith III
serves as a powder monkey at
Nanking in 1927

She knew a nice silk shop so we went it's a marvelous feeling
to go around in a rickshaw at first you think this is terrible but
then the rickshaw coolies were so gay

and merry and laughing and talking seemed to suffer no pain
seemed to enjoy themselves so you stopped feeling sorry for
them really you know except in your mind

Well you can tell in 15 minutes

if you think you're going to like them can't
you some people in five minutes you know
you're not going to like them you're surely as
smart as that you know perfectly well well all
right you could stay more you could stay half
an hour you could stay as long as you wanted
you could stay all afternoon sometimes you
weakened and had tea but it just depended
you kind of hoped they'd be out

Coffee ranks tea

In other words
Henry ranks your husband
so he does
he's alive

It amused me rather
it's like in my day many an admiral's wife
I've seen who's stalked ahead and sat in the
best seat well that's her right You're getting
into a steam launch with her and she gets in
plunks down that's her right she should

But we were not any more popular than nothing

    the missionaries kept pointing out that if we weren't there
    things would be peaceful and lovely
    it was our fault
    and Roy was terribly upset

    they were going to the Shanghai American School
    but his father said Now if you like you can take two friends
    down aboard ship I'll be home for the weekend You can go
    down and stay in my cabin You can have movies and be aboard
    ship

    to Roy age twelve a weekend on the ship was just heavenly
    he asked two friends first one and the other to his horror
    carried on as if he'd asked them to visit hell

schooling sea secretary-treasurer sent served service Shanghai she sister Smith Smith Commander Roy C. Jr. (USN (Ret) (USNA 1910) Smith Mary Taylor Alger Smith Montgomery M social social

How will I get home
I'm only telling you the alarming spots
I'm not telling you all the good spots

South Carolina states station stationed stays submarines superintendent support taken takes tells that the the the the to to

to her brother's chagrin dates
his company commander in
the early 1930s breaks her arm
as a child in Shanghai in the
mid-1920s meets third
husband in Newport after
WWII appearance causes stir
in Panama in the early 30s
education torpedo town

do loosen up your pen and pencil

the Panama scandal
the Hawaiian agitation
the Hawaiian question
the pardon
the horror
the financial crisis
the repeal
the mission
the visit
the blowing up
the war
our problems
the affairs
the death
the x-rays and wireless telegraphy
the bills
the death
the methods of teaching history
by which I mean each day is a pearl to be prized

And then one day

> to my enormous relief
> number one boy came upstairs
> Missy one piece long master
> have got One piece long
> master have got boy I fell
> down with excitement Then
> we stayed in Shanghai the
> children went to school like
> lepers as far as the
> missionaries were concerned

translates   typhoon   U.S.
uncomfortable   undesirable
unhappy   up   USN   (USNA
1880) USS King was when
while wife with wives word
World War I World War I
World War II

But what are you going to do with her

Put her in a closet can't put a curtain over her
head can you know what I mean they weren't
doing too hot well
                        they said it was follicular
lymphoma and in those days
                                    they told me he
would live just a few months maybe they told
him he was going to get fine and go back on
duty
            they told me remain cheerful and gay
don't tell your children say nothing to nobody
just remain normal
                        so he said to me well I
couldn't say so I put on as a bold show as I
could people use to say to me
                                    it's surprising
what you can do if you have to
                                    it's surprising
that's why these people that fall down and
can't get up all surprise me I bet you could
crawl to the phone if you had to
                                    maybe that'll
be my fate and I won't crawl to the phone I
don't know
                but we were only in Honolulu
for about a year just about a year and it was
lovely it was really lovely
                                it came to a very
quick and sad end it came to a quick and sad
end that's right

Acknowledgments

The language in these poems is found extensively through the erasure and collage of an oral history transcript from my great-grandmother, The Reminiscences of Mrs. Roy C. Smith, Jr. (U.S. Naval Institute, Annapolis, Maryland, 1986). Thank you to the U.S. Naval Institute for creating this record of my great-grandmother's life and permission to use the source text. This book is dedicated to my mother, grandmother, and great-grandmother.

Epigraph from "Imagining in Writing" By Robert Duncan, from *SELECTED POEMS*, copyright ©1950 by Robert Duncan. Reprinted by permission of New Directions Publishing Corp.

Thank you to The MacDowell Colony and the Djerassi Resident Artist Program for the time, support and space to begin and continue this book.

Thank you to Drew Kunz and Amber Bryant for publishing excerpts from this poem as the hand-bound chapbook *Boxer Rebellion* (g o n g press, Bainbridge Island).

Thank you to my Aunt Suzy Barnard for the stunning cover art. Thanks also to Dr. Evelyn M. Cherpak, Head of the Naval Historical Collection, now retired, at the Naval War College for photocopying and mailing many pages of my great-grandmother's letters for further research.

With gratitude and admiration for Myung Mi Kim, who read this manuscript at its inception in 1998 and told me to keep going; for Amaranth Borsuk, Don Mee Choi, Maryrose Larkin, Melanie Noel, Ed Smallfield, and for Kore Press, for their commitment to publishing women's writing. And always, for Paul Kimball and the Mangold-Stephens-Barnard contingent near and far for their love and support.

Sarah Mangold is the author of *Electrical Theories of Femininity* (Black Radish Books) and *Household Mechanics* (New Issues Press), selected by C. D. Wright for the New Issues Poetry Prize. The recipient of a 2013 National Endowment for the Arts Poetry Fellowship, she is also the recipient of residencies and fellowships from the Djerassi Resident Artists Program, the MacDowell Colony, Seattle Arts Commission, the Virginia Center for Creative Arts, and Willapa Bay AIR. From 2002—2009 she edited *Bird Dog*, a print journal of innovative writing and art. She received her BA in English Literature from the University of Oklahoma and MFA in Creative Writing from San Francisco State University. Originally from Oklahoma, she now lives and works in Seattle.

About the press

As a community of literary activists devoted to bringing forth a diversity of voices through works that meet the highest artistic standards, Kore Press publishes women's writing to deepen awareness and advance progressive social change.

Kore Press has been publishing the creative genius of women writers since 1993 to foster equitable public discourse and a diverse, accurate, historic record.

⚓ Since its inception in 1923, *Time Magazine* has had one female editor.

⚓ Since 1948, the Pulitzer Prize for Fiction has gone to forty two men and seventeen women.

⚓ Only twelve of 109 Nobel Prizes for Literature have gone to women. Three of the twelve female winners were in the last decade.

If you'd like to purchase a Kore Press book or make a tax-deductible contribution to the vital project of publishing contemporary women's literature, go to **korepress.org**